WATER AND THE LAND

Contents

Water all around us

Water is all around us.

▶This photograph shows a water chute at Aqua Land. Look at the shape that has been made for the water to flow down.

At Aqua Land, all the shapes were made by people. In the natural world, the water shapes the land. ▶

◀Can you see the shape that the water has made in the sand?

?

Are there any interesting or unusual shapes in the land near where you live?

Mountains, hills and lowlands

▶ Ben Nevis is the highest mountain in the UK. Ben Nevis often has snow on its <u>summit</u> even in the summer.

▼ Ely is a town on a hill. The hill is surrounded by very flat land called the <u>Fens</u>. Some of the land in the Fens is below <u>sea level</u>.

Can you find the Fens on the map of the UK on the opposite page?

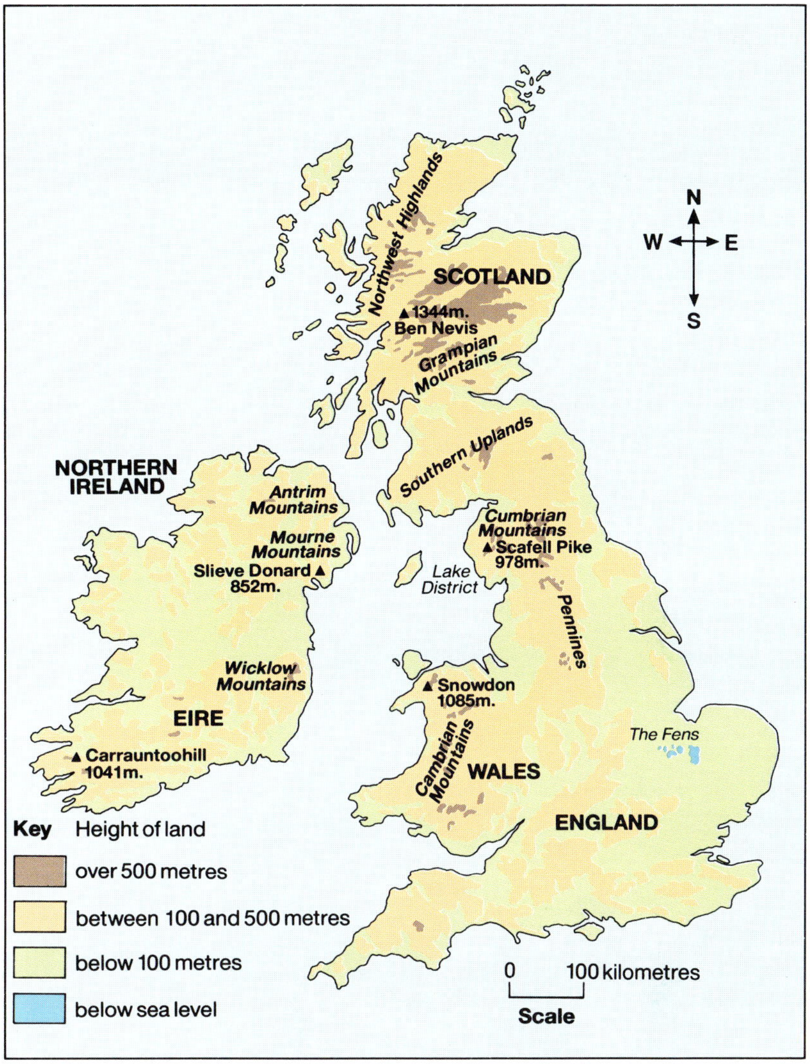

▶ The brown areas on this map are mainly mountains, the yellow areas are mainly hills and the green areas are the <u>lowlands</u>.

ACTIVITY

Find where you live on this map. Do you live in a lowland or a hilly place?

Write a description and draw pictures of a hill or mountain that you have visited, or seen in a book.

Living in the hills

▶ This photograph shows the Cheviot Hills. The Cheviot Hills are near the border between England and Scotland.

Look at the map on page 9. Find the Cheviot Hills and the border between England and Scotland.

▲ The black and white dogs in this photograph work on the farm.

What type of dogs are they? What do they do?

▼ Derek and Jennifer Charlton live on a farm in the Cheviot Hills. There are over 1,000 sheep on the farm. There are also some beef cattle and two cows.

In the winter, Derek and Jennifer have sometimes been 'snowed-in' for up to eight weeks. They are 11 kilometres from the nearest village. The nearest supermarket is at Alnwick, which is 24 kilometres away.

Imagine that you are 'snowed-in' at a country farm.
What problems do you think you would have?

ACTIVITY

Find how far it is from your own home to:

- the nearest shops
- a supermarket
- a post office
- a hospital
- a garage
- a railway station.

The Pennines

▼ The Pennine Mountains are called the 'backbone of England'. On the top of the mountains, the rainwater parts to go down one side of the mountain or the other. This is called a <u>watershed</u>.

A very long footpath called the Pennine Way follows this watershed in places. The south end of the Pennine Way is in Edale, Derbyshire. Look at the map on the opposite page. Can you find the north end of the Pennine Way?

When rain runs down the sides of hills, trickles of water join together to make streams. The streams join together to make rivers. A stream joining a river is called a <u>tributary</u>.

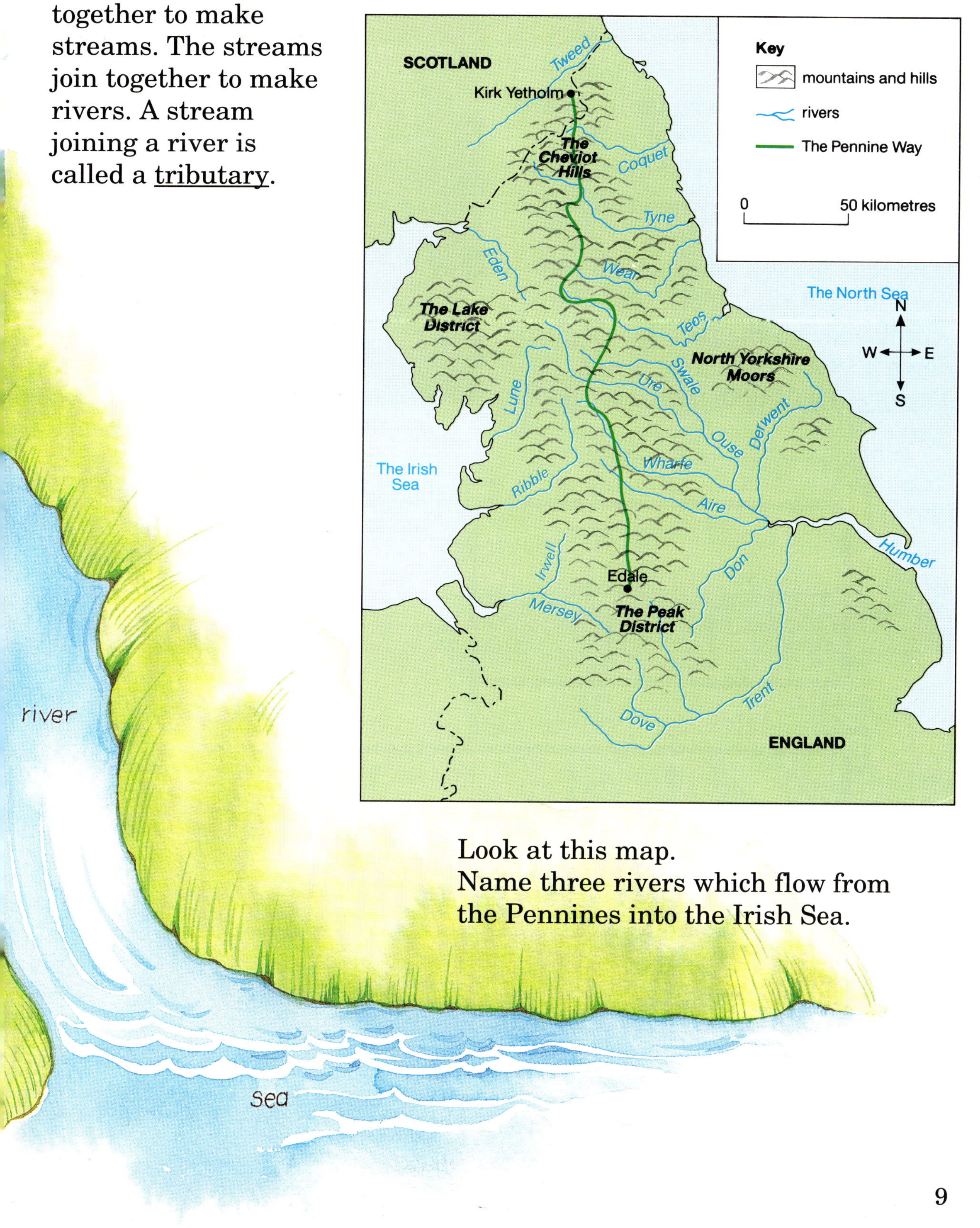

Look at this map.
Name three rivers which flow from the Pennines into the Irish Sea.

Where does rainwater go?

▶ Rebecca and Daniel's school used to have a flat roof. The builders are putting on a new pitched roof.

▼ This is a plan view showing how the school will look when the roof is finished.

The blue arrows show which way the rain will run off the roof. Rain will flow down the roof, into a gutter, down a spout and into a drain. The drain will take the water to a river.

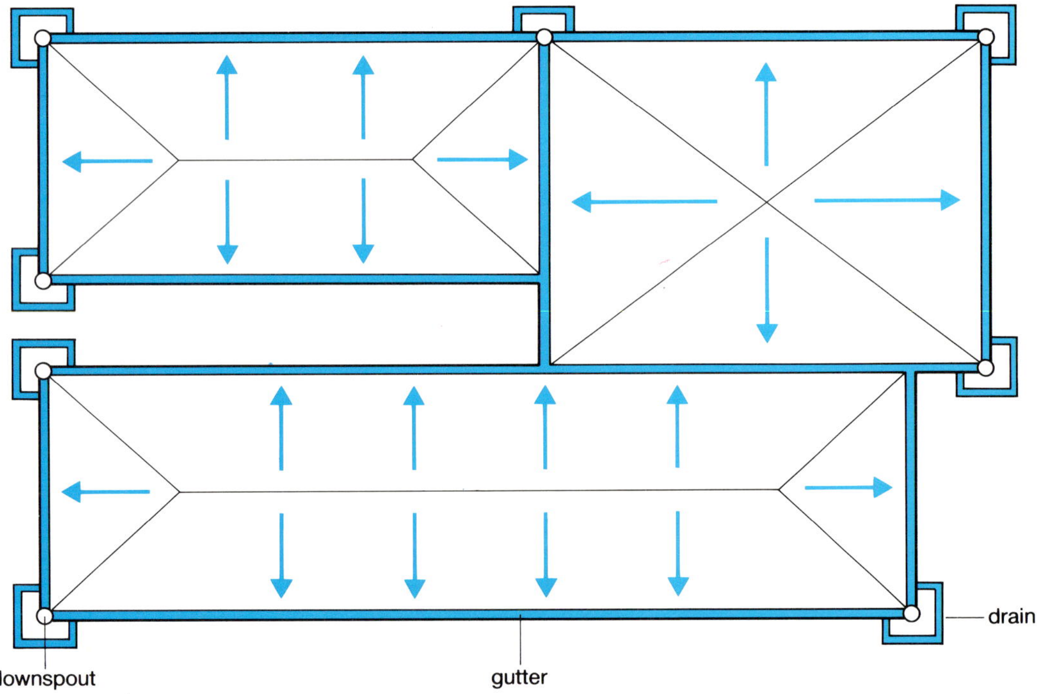

What sort of roof does your school have?
What happens when it rains?

Some rainwater soaks into the ground.

▼ Rebecca and Daniel wanted to find out if water soaks faster through clay or sand. They made two funnels from lemonade bottles. They put clay in one funnel and sand in the other. They poured the same amount of water on to the clay and the sand. After 30 minutes, they drew a black line on each bottle to show how much water had soaked through.

Which does rainwater soak through faster - clay or sand?

River valleys

The water in a river slowly wears away the ground that it flows over. This is called erosion. Little rivers make small valleys and big rivers make large valleys.

▲ This photograph shows the valley of the River Ribble in Lancashire.

▼ The photograph below shows the valley of Gordale Beck in the Yorkshire Dales.

▲ This is the Dee Valley and the River Dee in Scotland. The River Dee flows from the Grampian Highlands to the North Sea at Aberdeen. The river meanders in a wide valley.

◀ This is the Grand Canyon and the River Colorado in Arizona in the USA. The Grand Canyon is 2 kilometres deep.

In what way are these rivers and valleys the same?
In what ways are they different?

The Rivers Thames and Severn

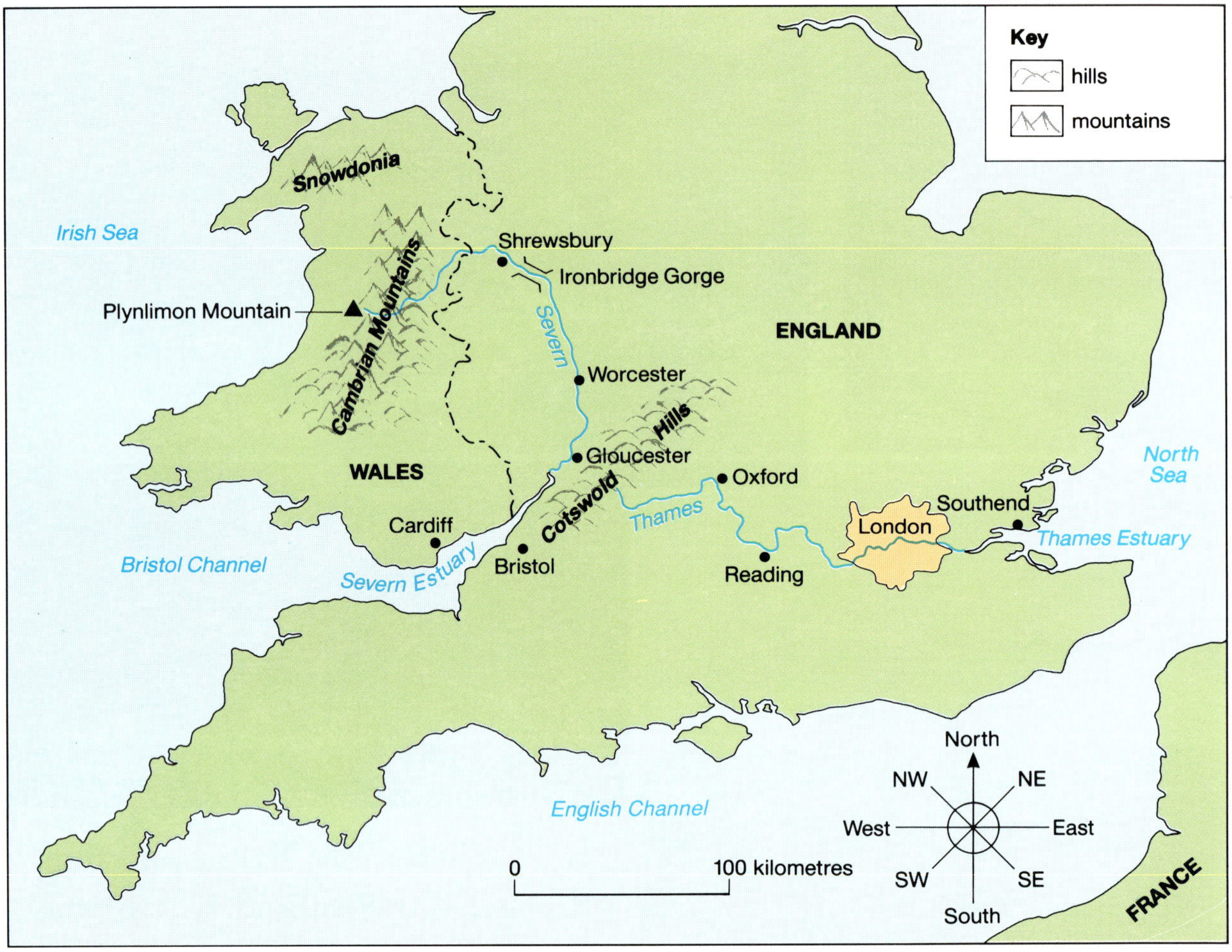

This map shows where the River Thames and the River Severn start and finish.

Where does the River Thames start?
Where does the River Severn start?
Which seas do the rivers flow into?

ACTIVITY

Find out the meaning of these words:
source, river mouth, estuary.
Now find out the name of the nearest river to your home.
Does it flow into another river or into the sea?

These photographs show the River Severn.

Which photograph shows the river near its source?

Which photograph shows the estuary?

Puddles, ponds, lakes and reservoirs

Do you like splashing in puddles? Have you ever wondered what happens to the water in puddles when the sun shines?

The air absorbs the water and the puddle dries up. This is called evaporation. The water from puddles and ponds can also soak into the ground.

▶Do you have a school pond? Find out from your teachers how it was made.

▼A lake is like a very large pond. Lakes fill hollows in the ground that have been worn away by erosion.

A reservoir is a lake made by people to store water. Reservoirs are made when a dam is built across a river. The water from the river collects behind the dam and the reservoir is formed.

▲ The photograph above shows the dam on the Clywedog River in Wales.

▶ This is Keilder Water, a reservoir in Northumberland. It is one of the largest reservoirs in northern Europe.

ACTIVITY

Find out more about reservoirs.
Why are they made?
What are they used for?

The seaside

Beaches are made from pieces of rock which have been broken down into pebbles and sand by the waves. This is another sort of erosion.

ACTIVITY

Collect some holiday postcards.

Sort out those which show beaches.

Find these places on a world map.

Now see if you can find more information on the places on the postcards.

▲ This is the beach at Eastbourne in Sussex.
◀ This is the beach at Gairloch in Scotland.

What things are the same about the beaches? What things are different?

Which sort of beach do you like best - pebble beaches or sandy beaches?

Water can be fun but it can also be dangerous. Sometimes it is polluted.

▼ This flag shows when the water at the seaside is safe and clean.

◀ Oil was spilt on this beach.

Can you see what is happening in the photograph?

The Amazon

Lots of different birds, animals and plants live in the Amazon Rain Forest in South America. Many of these animals and plants are dying because people are destroying the forest.

Farmers cut and burn down parts of the forest to grow crops or raise cattle. When this happens, the heavy rain slowly washes away the soil. Then the farmers burn down more forest.

What sort of river is the small river on the left of this photograph? (see page 9) Why do you think it is an orange colour?

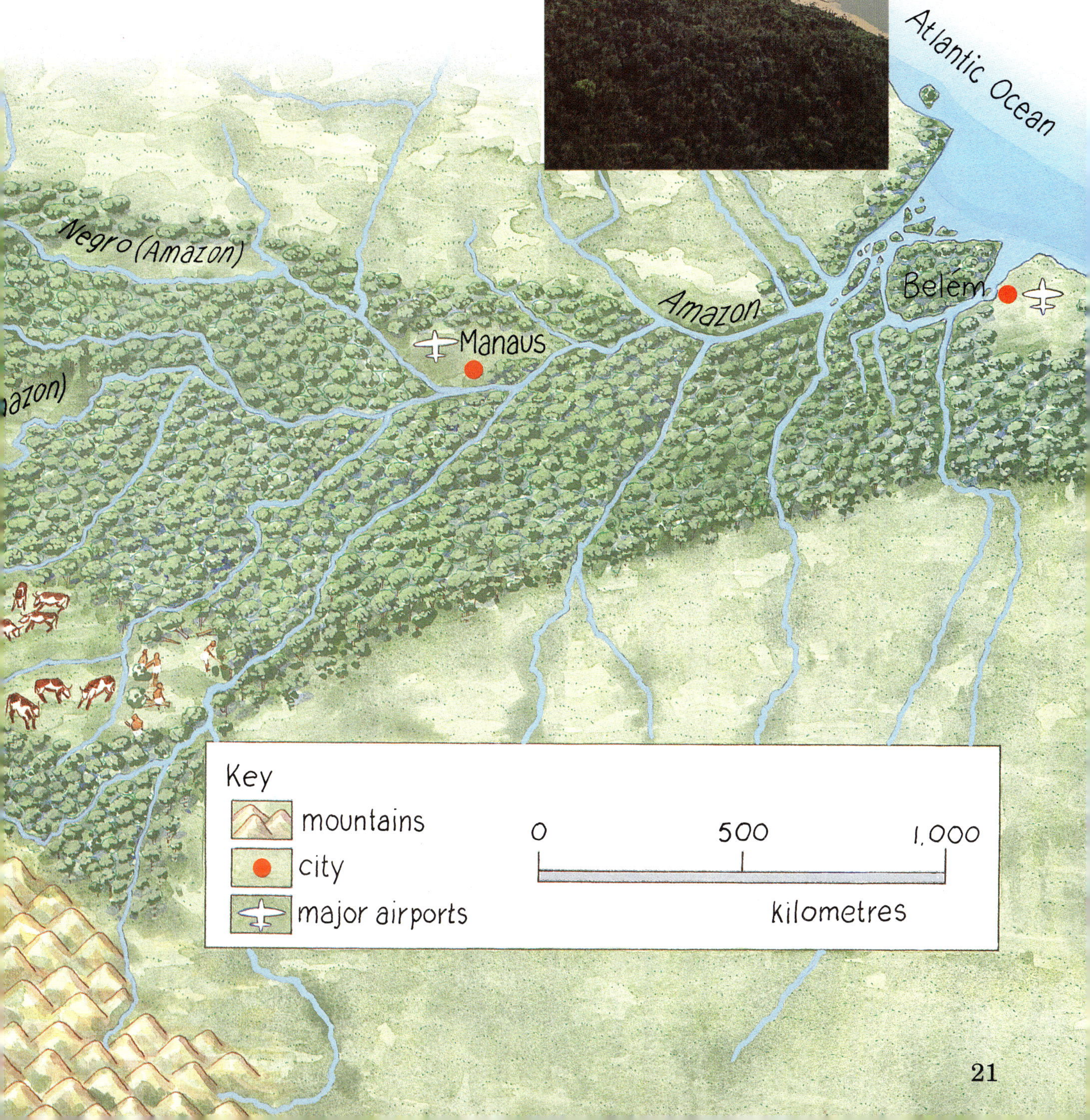

Living by the River Amazon

Maria and her brothers, Paulo and Miguel, live in a house on the bank of the River Amazon.

This part of Brazil is in the Tropics. There is no winter in the Tropics. It is hot every day and it rains a lot. During the wettest time of the year, the river floods some of the forest.

What is Maria's house made of? Why is it on stilts?

▼ There are no roads through the forest. The river is used for getting from one place to another. Maria's family have canoes to help them travel around.

▲ The river is also used for doing the family's washing!

▼ Maria's father grows vegetables and catches fish.

? **Where would you like to live - on a hill, near the seaside, or near a river?**

Glossary

These words are underlined in this book. This is what they mean.

absorbs
When something is absorbed, it is soaked up. For example, a sponge absorbs water.

erosion
This is what happens to the land as it is worn away by running water, wind and ice.

estuary
A river estuary is the place where the river flows into the sea. It is also called the mouth of the river.

evaporation
This is how a liquid, like water, turns into a gas, like air.

Fens
The Fens is an area of very flat land in the UK.

lowlands
Areas of flat land, like the Fens.

meanders
A river meanders when it flows in a curving bend.

mouth
The end of a river where it flows into a sea or lake.

polluted
When a river or sea is polluted, the water contains things which cause danger to people, plants and wildlife. Water can be polluted by things like rubbish, oil and other chemicals.

sea level
How high the sea is compared to the land.

source
The beginning of the river. The source is the place where it starts to flow.

summit
The highest point of a mountain.

tributary
A tributary is a small river which flows into a larger river.

Tropics
This is the part of the world between the lines called the Tropics of Cancer and Capricorn. The weather there is hot.

watershed
The place on the top of a mountain or hill where water parts to go down one side or the other.

Published by Cinnamon Press
Meirion House, Glan yr afon, Tanygrisiau,
Blaenau Ffestiniog, Gwynedd LL41 3SU
www.cinnamonpress.com

ISBN 978-1-905614-34-9
British Library Cataloguing in Publication Data. A CIP record for this book can be obtained from the British Library.

Designed and typeset in Palatino by Cinnamon Press
Cover design by Mike Fortune-Wood
Printed in Great Britain by Biddles Ltd, King's Lynn, Norfolk

Acknowledgements are due to the Editors of the various publications where versions of some of these poems first appeared: *Boundary; Coffee House Poetry; Crosscurrents; Envoi; Foreword for Poets; Moorlands Review; My Gun Is Bigger Than Yours; The Interpreter's House; Ouse Valley Poetry Competition 1996, Winners Anthology; Poets England 21 – Derbyshire; Poetry Monthly; Proof; Routemasters and Mushrooms, Earlyworks Press Poetry Anthology* (2006); *Salute To Outposts; Sepia; Staple; Success; Vigil; Westwords*

for Eileen,
who prefers the serious stuff

And if I laugh at any mortal thing,
'Tis that I may not weep.

Lord Byron, *Don Juan*

No Laughing Matter

Deaf-and-dumb man's hands

For Graham, for Jo

"Men of few words are the best men" - Shakespeare

Nails pared like syllables or labials
his hands are lean, tailored to efficiencies,
prepared for speed.

Looking at your eyes he sees you haven't grasped his sense
but, since there's little point in winging fingers into words,
allows his mouth to flounder over sounds.

Like un-ended sentences your hands hang
or, careless and extravagant, flap about like grounded birds
impotent to thread air's eloquence.

You stumble, too, at nuances of words
or, mouthing foolish vacuums,
shout in hope to rouse his sleeping ears.

He says, removed from friends with agile hands,
his fingers itch for conversation.

But, near to you, as limbs respond to what his fingers sing,
he knows his touch unlocks the meanings of your skin:
the silent dialogues of need, the speech of hands.

Hands for a Piano

i.m. GWN

My wife complains that playing Brahms demands
bigger hands than hers; and I remember yours:
not exactly large (like spades) but with limber fingers,
lean and strong; and recall how you wrung and rinsed
them at the front of class, or sat behind the teacher's
desk, and cricked finger joints, or made tepees spanning
against light, while we mastered adverbial clauses of time.

(You advised us, once, the best way to approach
an unknown score was through the andante
slow movement: *If that struck a chord,*
the rest would fall in line, in time.)

And I imagine you sitting in your prison cell,
humming the length of Brahms Piano Concerto 2,
and can see those hands laddering chords, taking the weights
of passion, nimbling the scales, but wonder what you did
as the cello sang solo in the slow movement.

Did you just sit, hands folded, fingers stilled,
counting time through bars?

Music Lessons

Hated scales, thumb-turning runs,
splitting-finger spans; dreaded the threatening
zebra keyboard, the measured metronome,
the rap of hands (*Keep those backs flat*); reeled
at room's chill and old food smell,
the piano-master's sawdust sleeve, his
next-to-woodyard reek; couldn't fit together
top and bottom lines, and was put
to songs that wouldn't/couldn't gel
(hark-harking larks, whistling o'er the lea)
yet keened for those vaster tunes
his mother rattled off or sang, those that
pulled his loins, stirred his guts...

So, this week's lesson finds him
in the copse, bike propped against a gate,
music-case idling amongst grass, where
from the score of trees he pulls together
the lark's grace-notes, the thrush's
sustained trill, the blow-flies' pedal-drone
held long time after flies have gone,
the ground-base of the zagging
blackbird crackerjacking through trees,
the bracken's spanning hands –

and all the time his yearning
bringing him the rhythms
of his *New World Symphony*

tunes he knows his mother understands...

Piano Lessons

Because she aspired to higher things
than other's uprights, my mother, while Dad's wealth
held, clung to a Bechstein baby grand –
a black-lacquered toad with sinister grin that squatted
in the lounge – at which, treading two brass tongues
she poured out music by the yard, and, because she thought
I ought to know how to play the piano, I was put to weekly
humiliation at some stranger's hands in a mausoleum-parlour,
all leatherette, cabbage smells and damp.

His was an upright like upended coffin with two
candle-brackets, an altarpiece to the priest of music,
with inlaid marquetry and obelisk of metronome
monumental as the room. There, ladders of scales took me
Step By Step To The Classics but the sound remained
grounded. It was like putting Meccano together, piece
by piece, so much undoing, tightening up, fitting a curve in;
or going to confession, repeating all last week's sins
by not practising what was preached. What I wanted was
tunes to wing (What did I care who Sylvia was?), not those
trills of notes like stranded tadpoles lying dried-up in nets,
so wangled out of lessons, and rejoiced when the Bechstein
gave up pride of place to a gramophone.

After years of going solo, achieving full *pianissimo*
in bars with trebles and Bass, I'm approaching *forte*,
so turn down the gramophone, and pick up duos
for four hands. I see there's sense in five-finger exercises,
spanning hands to execute bridge passages, and, despite
humiliation at some stranger's hands in Opus 1, I'm grounded
well in treading tongues in parlour and lounge, practised in
overtures, preludes, nocturnes, can accompany climaxes
without losing the rhythm, have found who Sylvia is,
and Rose (among the heather), not to mention several
easy pieces, some crochety or all of a quaver in semibriefs.
And though I've been known to run short of notes, I know
the score. I put it together, I confess, piece after piece –
undoing, tightening up, fitting a curve in – till, vamping
my way through life, I'm a regular upright man
fast becoming baby grand.

A Man There was Whose Alpha and Omega was Zed

For Bruno, for Ron

Zed was Zinaida, half-blood-bonded, put in charge
of schooling while the iron-master managed
jovially the Kamsko-Votinsk iron-mine;
she saw chasing after carriage that dragged mother
away; saw clinging to wheels, pleading after melting face.

Zed was Zaremba, proprietor of German counterpoint,
forging notes to scales, tempering harmony,
firing/refining/steeling the young man's mind
but not finding *Winter Day Dreams* white-hot enough.

Zed was Zhukovsky, translator of Joan's visions
to a death deprived of a cross, and, after the final stake
of imagined fire, a resurrection of twenty-four curtain-calls.

Zed was NadeZhda, almost centralized letter-headed benevolence,
passing distantly in parks, in carriages,
with no words but written
wanting progeny of no blood,
beloved friend, true Tatyana of the letter-scene.

Zed was zigzag of doubt, mark of self-awareness,
the secret, the guilt,
the millstone of *Onegin*, ground on the gritstone
of marriage where his Zedness wouldn't grind.

Zed was N on the side, never face to face,
a no-kid creator, though lover of kids.

Zed was Zvierev, funeralled in friendship,
and leaning (pathetically) over St. Petersburg
in rehearsal for an own death of final *adagio lamentoso.*

Zed was the cholera-zygoma of a mother with expressive eyes,
and the cholera-escape of a man with eyes prone to crying.

Botanical Eve

Pale Flax, Lady's Tresses, Hairgrass.
Oxeye, Eyebright.
Sneezewort.
Toothwort.
Oxlip.

Nipplewort and Milkwort:
Mollyblobs.

Lungwort
Liverwort
Kidney Vetch.

Spleenwort
Bladderwort.

Privets
Goatsbeard
Figwort
Downywoundwort.

Snakeweed, Snakeroot
Hairy Stonecrop.

Creepingtwitch
Touch-me-not
Creepingtwitch and Creepingtwitch.

Lady's Bedstraw.

Spearwort.
Softrush,
Hardrush, Jointed Rush.
Saxifrage.

Traveller's Joy and Speedwell.

Quaking Grass, Wildthyme, Loosestrife.

Love-in-a-mist, Love-in-a-mist.

Heartsease.

Rue. Heartsease. Rue.
Rue Rue Rue.

Forget-me-not,
Forget-me-not,

FORGET-ME-NOT.

October Evening

is enchantment

paling sun leans faintly
rays angling away
shadows grown thin
clouds pulled ribboning out

(so many strands
so many skeins)

and everywhere
the silver litter of spiders
like fine hair
whisped in shimmered light

(leans angling thin
pulled ribboning out
so many strands)

to enter it
is to approach Eve's temptation

feel how broken
it lingering clings

(so many skeins)

and in the morning has taken up
new places, new perfection

and innocence hangs on air

(fine lingering clings)

conspires seduction everywhere

(approach temptation
enter perfection)

Eve's Lament

Krishna, come, come soon.

He, being dark blue,
has always been
my favourite god;

For, when his mother
told him off for eating mud,
he opened his mouth
and she beheld
the entire universe.

Krishna, come, come soon.
Come soon
and show me your face.

Astral Projections

I Our fuel bills are costing us
the earth.

II All that about character and stars
is not a load of bull:
my sister's Taurus,
and she's a right cow.

III We've considered solar energy:
it's nearly as cheap as *The Sun*.

President For Life

There's never an escape:
name on statue, name on bust,
on square, on plaque, on street,
and in your pocket/purse/wallet
name on the 5000 dinar note

The long concrete spans
linking Krk to the mainland
underpin his presence

Land weighed down with the spell
of his name spelled out in patterns
of stone like some post-war menhirs
dragged from abandoned randomness
to be marshalled on hillsides
wherever you look in letters
bigger like him than man

TITO TITO TITO

Some sentence he served

Even death
won't let him
off the hook

Relics

I have suddenly become collectable.

My nose was taken at Nimes and again
in Berlin, and rests now in Bradford and Rouen;
my left leg was swooped on by an American
just outside the great west door of Notre Dame.

My head graces many places from Lucerne
to Japan (just think on that St John);
and my trunk's snapped like the antiquities of Rome,
while my backside's the pride of many a collection.

I've more big toes than Saints Peter and Paul.
Like Venus de Milo I've lost both my arms.
I must have Michelangelo's David's charms,
for some folks I know have my torso whole.

Is this the beginning of a new religion
to rival the frieze of the Parthenon?
Rest assured, I shan't want anything back:
take my indulgence – you can keep it all with Kodak.

This is southern Spain

And he with the Aztec-patterned sweat shirt,
Grecian 2000 and brylcreemed parting
and she with her firm perm and sensible sandals
are def-in-ite-ly English

He crosses the grass,
handles the span of a succulent
as wide as her thigh
then fingers its spindly leaf-bud
lingeringly

She pads off to coffee
con leche – naturally

Sparrows wing to lechery
in the broken mill

Grecian still-life

While she lies sunbathing
dreaming of grandchildren

and he lies quietly trying
to melt into the chilled marble
so as to deflect his thoughts from sex

the tiger-striped wasp
feasts itself on the damsel-fly's carapace.

Landscape Painting

witnessed in

road-mauled hares
whose fresh torn guts twitch nervously

towers of foxgloves
stabbing spears against the sky

ox-eyed rosettes
stiffly held beneath grazing rains

trodden buttercups
whose underneaths stream silent gold

burnished oaks
aching into life, dying to live

razored thrushes
sharing worms' warm blood

evening's wounded suns
spilling into pink clouds

sharing one scene

Still life till end.

Highways Maintenance – The Poet on Work Experience

This week it's digging ditches, and I've been assigned to Jack.
He doesn't banter much – has got his fags so rarely mithers
me but stands there, grins and smokes, or takes a casual hack
at last year's rioting weed, while I nick the ground, cutting back
clean, straight lines for the water-course from weather's
crumblings, so hill-springs can resume their former route.

The spade is Jack's: semi-circular, ugly-looking brute,
more of a grimace than a smile, honed and keen-edged
by use. To start, it's a soft thud into roots, instep wedged
against the blade, and strength shared out between a lunge
from somewhere just above the groin but beneath the waist,
till the quag of soil spits, sucks, gives and wets like sponge.
Next the lift, all the time willing mud to stay complete,
fingers-crossed it won't collapse on self. For a really clean cut,
one straight swing is best. Speed helps. To hesitate
is to give the sludge reason to rebel. Afterwards, a neat
backwards arc, taken steadily, then a slight, twisting knock
and off the stoppage slides on grass – it's a piece of cake! –
wedges of it castellate the verge at regular treads.
Each one's a year's cross-section: the road's caviar-grit,
the rich humus, the moth's laced wings suddenly caught
in slush, and, now, the anaemic veins of springing seeds:
a geology of growth striated in this gulleying aqueduct.

I marvel at this trench, and what the hedge confirms:
the shrew's bleached skull, the kestrel's yesterday snacks,
lean bones, moles strung on the barbed-wire's cruciform,
the catkin's citrine swinging. All this is beyond Jack's
understanding. Knowing his real strengths lie with tarmacs
not ditches and drains, I suffer silently his smokes and grins.
The sum of our differences is this: while he covers up cracks
to keep them down, I dig deep to reveal the bottom of things.

Hedging

I

Farmer Warren
lean as the wind
is on to a good thing

For when he clips
the hawthorns round his fields
they do not even raise
one finger against him

yet when I try
to prize my children's toys
from between their stems
their hands reach out to scratch me

It is my blood, not his,
which nourishes their autumn berries

II

Though Tom sees April is crimson-tipped, a madder-brown
giving way to filigrees of green quickthorn
and ascensions of pale Mayflowers
with maudlin smells ghosting down lanes in search of summer,
he knows from his aching hands and the lacy ground
that still through the hawthorn blows the cold wind

III

Autumn's warning rings through the chill lane:
Tom's at the hawthorn again.
His hands inherit the rhythm of the land: a ritual
as hatchet snags at straggly lateral

polled swing lop chip rend

Habits rooted hedge-deep, face all berry-red,
back angled against wind, bowed his head,
and hands knotted like the limbs he hacks,
his skill is grafted from his granddad's past

hold swing lop chop tend

Now comes the laying. Angling to the left,
a twenty degrees lean that splinters cleft
of wound where clear sap bleeds, he weaves the limbs
and lashes them with whippy ends of stems

fold cling lap slip blend

Done now, he cleans his blade, wipes smears of green.
Beneath his boots tread crowns of cut-down thorn
he piles to snappy crackling pyres.
In hedgerows foxgloves lean their pietas

tolled swing droop stoop bend

through the sharp hawthorn blows the cold wind

Peak District Highways

In late March, ignoring the spring-frisky cows' quizzical gaze,
they rise between flags of grass, pale furls of fern
and stitchwort unpicking its milky knots
to thread a counterpoint to the stream's equivocal turnings,
the whirring pheasants and the cronking grouse.

> Who paves their progress, scattering horseshoe hoops,
> the linnet's eggs, the magpie's piebald quill,
> the shrew's littered skull?

In July, busy at their meanderings,
they scrub the bilberry bones, subtract the heather's abacus,
the mica's sliding silt, and huddle where the curlew whets its bill
between the foxglove's leaning towers
and the hawthorns in the dell.

> Who betrays their confidences? Their whisperings?
> Their ancient cabalas?
> Who scores their stillness? Their song?

On honey-coloured September mornings, when moorscapes
suddenly own to honesty, they rehearse their alibis,
skirt the fields in Indian file, ambush the elderberry's
bloody shot and bramble's angry coils,
then lose the track in conundrums of cricket-stump stiles.

> Who writes their itineraries?
> Draws up their meeting place?
> Directs their crossroads?
> Plans that head-on rendezvous?

On December days, when skies grow purple under hanging clouds
and earth is deceived by tricks of snow and sleet
or drifts outsculpting Henry Moore, they're declivities
dogging the wall with its chapped stone grit
or following the crow's frozen road, the fox's trotting trail.

From what do they gain their purposes
these moorland lanes? What drives their perspective?
Informs their shocking views? Their ends?

God only knows.

Carsington Water,
September Sunday Afternoon

Parking the car, we trekked through autumn woods
whose bracken fronds our hissing kids imagined snakes.
(We joined their game, but hoped they didn't cry wolf.)

Through copper light, dappled by beech leaves
spiralling on air, we saw the waste of water mimicking the day.

It drew us. If others hadn't similarly been drawn
we would have fallen, as grass kept feet guessing
where they were safest placed.

Soon at the shore, lake lapping a domestic dog
its wet nose pushing to a game of throw and fetch
that shoved up twisted sticks at our Sunday shoes
and urged our joining in.

We threw. And laughed at slapping coots squabbling
for safety among the reeds; but didn't share their fear.
Nor had much pity for a bloated roach, belly sickening white:
we only felt the stench, while everywhere sliding leaves
perspired our overthrow.

Soon the sun, sucked out of warmth, dipped behind trees
whose fingerings released chill breeze and clutched too many gnats
for peace of mind, or hand.

By now the lake (a devious cheat, too animal to bring back
sticks) had grown two-faced with fishy goings-on we couldn't
penetrate though anglers plumbed its mind.
We only knew it killed,
already had some boats and yachts upkeeled.

Hurriedly we pulled the kids back through trees;
now found their hissing game unbearable
but were so intent on keeping peace to reprimand,
and more proud to admit to them and selves
that we'd much preferred the after-dinner film,
so reluctantly replied *Yes, we'll come again.*

A Cromford Piece

Arkwright might well be surprised to learn his
Cradle of Industrial Revolution that
Rocked him to fame (while children tumbled,
Over-tired, to early graves, and exhausted
Men and women sweated in the deafening clangs
From water-frame and spinning-jenny) has
Outlived two hundred years and still stands,
Redoubt-like, behind its towering walls.
Doubtless, though, he wouldn't begin to understand how
Politics have fashioned Cromford's decline to sideline his
Inventive skills till his mill's grandeur is reduced to
Exhibition space, silent rooms, or rash of shops where
Coach-loads of folk pick over imported clothes made
Even cheaper in the Far East's sweatier shops.

Even to the second and third generation

Looking at his only grandson, a six-year him,
his eyes' pride lets my wife's dad's secret out the bag:
he wanted her, his only child, to be a lad.
Luckily for her she's not concerned at all
and, living with me, is glad to have his practical skill:
she hangs paper plumb, paints doors more readily
than lips, screws well and good,
but still is heavenly-feminine.
I have no fear for her: she aids my husbandry.

But, my James – sometimes, I fear for him.
It's not his fingers fattening round the tools,
calloused trophies on his hands, blisters on his thumb,
chips, nicks and cuts in his pearly skin,
or his hammers, drivers, chisels, rules
and saws – it's not all this (for after all,
He is a lad, and screwing just comes naturally),
but squaring it with what he's got from me.

So, when, in his books, he sees Humpty falling off the wall
and sad-eyed enquires *What colour are eggs' blood?*
while his mum smiles, and granddad laughs out loud,
I chill and squirm inside. For me his grammar's less concern
than his connecting lines.
Those chromosomes and genes
have lots for which they're answerable.

(Or, perhaps, my dad
would rather I'd have been a girl...)

Arms and A Boy

Bump, and in he comes, my son, my six-year-old lump
of boydom, trundling through the door, his arms
a heaving sheaf of blue, so full the colour hides his eyes.
Bluebells, Mum and the pulled stems bundle in my hands.
Unlike him, they're lean and thin, their greenness
seeping anaemically to white where light has never seen before
and sap is dripping down his grubby nails.
Heavy with flower, their heads hang with bells
of fragile blues that smudge to purple at their rims.
The only sound they ring is scent that drowns the dining-room.

Been stung he boasts, then keens. And thrusts his knee
with its perfect nettle-mounds, white-islands in the smear
of dock leaves he hurriedly applied. But it's Mum
he needs. As I apply the calamine, he rubs his cheek
against my dangling hair, and puts his arms around my neck.
Then, leaving me with foolish swabs of cotton-wool, he
rushes out to terrorize the garden with his gun.

How can I explain to him his gift would better be
if left to grow, when in the lounge I arrange chrysanthemums
his father's brought? And how offset the hope that when
he's grown he'll have no need for gun, with expectation
that as a man he'll greet his Mum with larger arms
that spill with cultivated blooms? Bemused, I plunge
his present in a glass, and start the tea. He is so young.

At times like these you have to play the game; forget hypocrisy.

Occupation

Haircuts were short of course
and butter disappeared
and people died of starvation
occasionally
but the children got on
jolly well with the soldiers.

Game of Consequences

You sidetrack your twelve-year-old son
from wanting a *Star Wars* Mega-bike
like, at eight, you distract him from a laser-gun,
or, at four, you explain all death away. The trick?
Not using words (they're merely signs of signs);
but shrug and fudge, lie with smiles, or pick
up paper, fold, and fold, and with his rainbow-crayons,
draw some party monsters. It's called *being politic.*

You sidetrack your twelve-year-old son
from needing a *Star Wars* Mega-bike like
you deal with your girl, suddenly seventeen,
taking A Levels, and going philosophic
as fears mushroom on her young-woman horizon:
AIDS, the dole, the bomb. Calling it *Knowing for the sake*
of knowing, you fake hope, change tack, and as a final distraction,
propose she throws a monstrous party. Being politic

you sidetrack your twelve-year-old son
from having a *Star Wars* Mega-bike like
you convince yourself buying-up early Haydn
symphonies for your old age: *Time's elastic, like*
this music, son. Things fall in and out of fashion.
It's how you want/need/have your art. You fake
facts, fold truths on truths, clutch hope: distraction
almost as glib as party politics.

Riding A Bike

For Locker

Being purist and wanting
to get back to first principles
and cut against the accretions
of centuries of translation –
the shades of meaning, nuances
of words – and so get to language's
roots, he took up Bede thinking
that, Latin primer by his side,
he could con the text and,
like riding a bike,
back would come Catullus
even though at first the wheels
might wobble away as he rode.

Hadn't reckoned with the need
to reinvent the wheel.

What's the Latin for bike?

Wedding Song

He liked her eyes: they reminded him
of the colour of starling's eggs, and clear winter skies.
She liked his eyes, also: big and brown as chestnuts;
but had to confess she was fearful of birds.

He admired the neat way her neat nose
defined her face, and the pleatings of her smiles.
She warmed to his broad nose; his wide grin.

He loved her fine hands, and the way she'd made them good
in the kitchen, with baking and cakes.
She traded his kitchen-clumsiness for his tenderness
with fish, his skill in handling frogs.

He liked her child-likeness; her sense of fun;
her oh-so-muchful-noisiness (especially in singing);
her innocence. He found all of this comforting.
She grew used to his quest for facts; his search for truth;
his challenging attitude; his openness. It fascinated her.

He wanted her homeliness; her creating of place;
her attempts to organize him; her bossiness.
He wouldn't change this for the world.
She tolerated his cigarettes; his poor time-keeping;
the fact that he wore his clothes un-ironed.
She'd make sure some things were changed.
She knew she would.

So, this couple, decked in fine clothes and flowers,
posed for photos with families and friends; allowed
gifts, good wishes and advice to be showered on them;
and, warming to the role of groom-and-bride, exchanged
wedding rings, made solemn vows, and promised
to honour and love for the rest of their lives.

It was a full day, big with laughter and friendship.
(And some tears.)
In fact, everyone agreed, it had been a dream of a day.

And, in the morning, they woke
to become
husband and wife.

Circles of Insanity

In the rain autumnal, steadily down-pouring,
and the trees, the elms with leaves descending,
I madam, have brought them,
your daughter and hers, to see you, gold with age,
to take you away, circling and reeling,
confusing the birds with this burnt snowfall.

And alone I sit meditating sanity,
listening to the rain seeping and the feeting
of the lack-eyed man fenced away wheeling
his way circular through the trees,
calling the world with akimbo-ed arm,
I think, for turning him here sadly
and yelping, yelping with the sinister crow,
I am mad, of the fingered wing
defining insanity.
                                        And on the wall
the fussing sparrows *hop hop hopping* go,
then circle the leaves and share the knowledge
in the steady autumnal rain and the trees
that I have brought them, madam.

Helen at Seventy

is becoming bird.

Eyes liquid-alert to inroad:
her defensive glances
pin others to their distances.

Hearing gone, head atilt,
she listens with her watery sight;
shoulders stooping, her back round,
she hunches at her food's stabbing ground.

Words chittering a repetitive drill,
her speech croaks, tapping out
sentences of the present
from the syntax of the past.

Nails thick and scored
her hands grow raw chicken claws.
Hair feathering to skins,
her head's shrunken to skeletal eloquence.

Beakish her nose.
Her legs are spindling to veins.
Her fledglings gone.
Her hands a last year raggy nest.

Though for now she roosts, eyes closed,
knows she'll soon wing into flight:

an angelic bird of paradise.

New Year Resolution

Hostile day. Wind lean. Light toothed.
Land locked in struggle.

After almost two months of this
everything is on the edge of surrendering
to cold's stranglehold.
They've all had more than they can stand,
all that is, save the wild dog-rose.

From beneath crushing weights of snow,
the squeeze of ice, the press of frost,
it flexes barbs,
restrings limbs
and boasts
Thank god, being self-sufficient, I can exist.
Will never give in.

Knows that in pursuit of being, it must suffer,
must accept all that weather has to offer.
That to prosper it must fight
        to drink deeply must deny thirst
        to stay alive must bleed to death.

Otherwise there can be no continuing,
no chance to re-enter,
no rebirth.

Along with earth is resolved
to be here at the end.

First of March

and the snowdrop
          petals browning at lips,
          leaves spilling out a tangled mop,
          head dragging leadenly out of sky's reach
is proud to have pulled through
despite the drilling cold.

It cannot take any more
so pleading earth for release
complains of exhaustion,
begins to negotiate.

The payment is self
and the fulfilment of self.

That can only be when it's burnt out,
a used squib,
done through.

So must suffer while crocuses blaze.

But thrills that at earth's mouth
darkness waits.

That's some consolation:

to be wanted.

Midnight March in the mist

And up on the moor it is dark:
the sky has misplaced the stars and moon
and only has low clouds to show for itself.

It is that dark that the road empties
his pockets to inspect its secrets.
They spill out at our feet
so much flotsam and jetsam
we've not seen the like before.

But the road is safe:
our words are inadequate to tell what we see
and what's more there's not even cats' eyes
to split on him.

Open-mouthed, gateways stand further back
than we remember as amazed we mistake
the bent oak and its crow's nest
for a shift in the mist.

Even the houses have lifted their anchors.
Stone walls loom out in front of us,
seem bigger, grander as they roll
one after the other like faceless waves.

The moor is ocean once more.

The waves of clouds fall down on us,
the tides of mist edge and lap
and the road is reduced to shingle –
Chesil Bank uprooted.

It is so alien that to reassert locality
our feet feel through the bottom of shoes
and search for the hardness of land,
the reassurance of soil.

With no guiding light we nudge along
consoling ourselves with promises of arrival
and home.

In fact, it's as well
night has a long memory
and can recall when all this was submarine
for without him to navigate
we'd be completely at sea.

June

Is the same as May, but fuller

The same tree is the same as the same tree in May, but fuller
Its arms are the same, and its twigs
And its topmost heads are the same, but fuller
And its underneath shade is pools of the same, but fuller

And fuller the sky with insect wings and wings of birds
Fuller the clouds with rain and the bare blue light fuller
The nests and hedgerows fuller fuller
The sheeps' bleat and the curlews' beat fuller
The fields, the flowers, the heads of grass, fuller and fuller

The whole thing fuller
The month like a man at a seasonal feast
With each mouthful fuller and fuller
Fit almost to burst

The whole month screaming *fuller* ***fuller*** ***fuller***
It can't get enough

Except the bones underneath
Where moor shrinks her limbs to the lean stone walls
And her desperate screams come ***smaller***
smaller
smaller

Sounds for Sunbathing in a June Afternoon Garden

Beech leaves rehearse whispers of shingle.

Spaced farms apart, cockerels are playing Queenie-I-Koko.

A far dog rasps sawing planks.

Next door's spade filling barrows with gravel
Shunts, chugs and spouts between runs.

A maxim mower strafes down the lawn.
Overhead, starlings scramble a tangled cassette tape;
Suzukiing to Silverstone, fruit flies let throttles rip full out;
Bees kamikaze among pearl arbours of hawthorn.

Cuckoos protest *love you, love you*.

Won't someone answer the ringdove's telephone

Or are you deafened by the rose-petal's fall.

White Foxglove

I

Lulled by stream's crystal divinity
of seepage beneath the moor's rim,
I drank myself blind on water
and the sounds of water, the chirrings

till suddenly woke
to your six-foot-or-more perpendicular
flower-arrangement that you've made
from yourself and the full bowl of your foliage
for earth's altar.

II

Ascensions of green seed-packets –
each a chalice to propitiation –
grace the place that makes your calendar of growth
as you've hauled yourself together
above the tall grass, the leaf-mould

and, higher still, tiered choirs of bells
each peal a miniature of the row before
and lightened by a brighter green –
image of what remains in flower
or deigns to bloom:
living yuletide decoration
honouring the wrong solstice.

III

Looking again, I drink in the whole of you
with twinned side-shoot replicas –
deeped, angled at your foot – your own scale models
like an Old Master martyrdom
with central gibbet framed between lesser deaths.

IV

Pulled from only looking
I touch your pouting lips,
run finger-tip between
silvered filaments refracted to diamond
and unlock your womanhood,

your o-ness leading to womb reach,
the green blotches beneath creamy-white ceiling
that blushes to progeny,
your stigma-clitoris brushed
between the wild bee's kneading:

Albino daughter of Albion –

girl of this earth rising to die.

Field Poppies

are better copies of their paper images,
more tissue-thin than their imitators.

Seen from a distance banked together
where wounds are carved, soil humped
for new roads, homes and clay growing tall –
such rich harvest out of so much dust –
you could mistake them for docks
they so resemble rust.

But looked at close in isolation
each open face leaning to the sun
there's no mistaking them
they're so many shades of the same red.

They've been patiently waiting
keeping their gritseed energy latent
till pushed into revealing all.

Now dragging out of moor's deep
where they've lain blind, drugged, asleep
they're mouthing the memories of centuries
with midsummer bloods that smudge the verges
and nightmares that cannot race away.

Like soil, they thrive on disturbings.

Cyclamens

Lovely-ugly buds flamingoing
from leaf-pools; one-legged-erect
to lift in wings of flowers.

Or white-veiled, a leaning grace
of flustered nuns rushing to vespers,
quietly, quietly.

Bird or saint, bird and saint
(both earth-footed, dark-rooted)
are angels crusading,

eyes fixed on sky,

each to its own God
each in its own cause:

living to die.

Gentians

Follow your eye through an autumn morning.
Notice mists lingering round fingers of fir, silver wisps
caught on auburn leaves. Think this garden is September-sad,
suddenly old with threads of web, the hedge beginning to thin
though summer's remnants have come to a head
and Michaelmas is memory of best times past.

Amidst all this, focus on a pull of blues
striped with skeins of cloud as gentians cling to summer skies.
See them set against the light, like Favrille glass,
fine and fragile, or mouthing at the sun their heads swelled bells
like gaudy Christmas balls;
or at your feet as if peacocks shedding eyes stepped across this grass.

Touching them, feel their skins silky in your hands:
thins of ribbon, the last-ditch-campaigner's flash
of autumn warring against chilling winds.
At dusk, remark their closing, like balloons stolen home from dances
that, after kids have done, sag away to become
flat blue bags of trash.

Recall, for fifty weeks they retain a memory of blue:
in their roots, in your mind.

Know then how near to you
fear of darkness reaches out before, behind.

Acorns

are October impostors posing as stones;
masqueraders parading their polished exteriors;
nests of pebbles lying below boles of oaks

They've got it down to perfection:
rounded, marbled, smooth –
their ambition cocooned, purpose concealed

They don't want all the year's sacrifice lost in one bite,
have been warned to be fearful of teeth,
so push snuggling downwards,
away from the sluggish dormouse, the marauding squirrel

Looking up at that vast oak
such massiveness, such gnarled bark, such twisted limbs,
so much tree,
seems incompatible with such a small pearl-seed

Now errant gems
they search for security:
a pale start that will flourish into magnificent gestures,
embracing soil, and ground,
nets for fingers, nets for roots

Possessors
Possessors

by posing as innocents

Alderley Woods, November the First

i.m. Howard Sergeant

The year is burning itself to an end.
A larch leans, its spindles yellow-celandine.
Beech leaves drift like amber sand:
it's the sea's swell you imagine
and shingle fingering the shoreline.

Mustard-powder-dry are the tops of the far copse.
What remains is lichenous or dried sphagnum moss.
The oak is ochred, the chestnut turned rust.
In the colour of leaves, and the smoke from the woodburner's fire
there is cinnamon, nutmeg and ginger here.

The birch bole is ashen and limed,
and a maple with its lemon edges amazes its neighbour.
Hush, hush says the wind.
I'm always red claims the acer
dismissing the crimson-tipped sycamore.

With barely a skein of cloud, the sky is wide and clean.
The sun hangs low, albino.
The wood-dove flies a rainbow,
while, high in the elm, magpies cackle alarm
as the falcon stoops down.

In a light that is chill and thin
between nettles' leggy stems,
above bracken hands (flat and golden),
stinkhorn's glans, and acorn's pebbly gems
gnats scrabble a crossword, across and then down.

And there, hugging the rhythm of land
where the harvest's been gleaned, spears
of grass, tipping the seed-drill's militia
are bringing the certain Spring.

Lilac in November

For Erica

Heavy frost last night: ground whited over, crystalline.
And this morning, air brittled and chilled; light thin.

From this window, a high wall, six foot away,
limiting vision. Some bricks still tipped with frost,
cushions of moss with vermillion antlers making inroads
on mortar. The red face shales away in parts.

Against flaking brick, limbs of lilac, leaves long blown,
now green-limed and bare, or madder-brown and bare,
limbs that from a bole grown middle-aged, and smoothly rotund,
rehearse a twisted stairway to where the wind rocks,
leaning to thins of fingers and sky's nothingness.

Already it wears next spring's buds:
triangular crowns that deep inside greenness
hide pyramids of upturned grape straining to burst open-faced:
purpling fists of bloom bruising Mayday airs with draping fragrances.

With the worst of this year still to come,
such certainty alarms, such abundant trust disarms.

Willow-herb

Saw them first: a pink blush
that lay flushing the railway siding –
a haze defining the lie of the track.

Too massy, too pink to be foxgloves –
though almost as tall, as finger-thin –
they flanked the embankment.

Nearer, it was the spearmint green
of leaf and stem that mattered –
though didn't displace the rose-glow
of open-mouthed florets, their eye-white
centre, their silence.

Some already had gone grey –
fading palely – seed-heads flocking
like dandelion clocks, borrowing the breeze
and planning inheritance.

Willow-herb – rose-bay willow-herb –
memories of fresh horizons, lost youth.

No Laughing Matter

There was this woman, this man named Percy, and this parrot…

Not parrot, actually, but macaw some wag had called Micawber;
not Percy's either though he'd motored miles to bring it back,
but Great Aunt Annie's who always had stacks of ready cash.

Just like Giles' cartoon Granny, with manky fox-fur wrap
that snapped our worming fingers, she was a one for jokes:
could pull almost all herself apart. Had those tricks with sliding
thumbs and stolen noses; would let her false bun fall then jig it in
our faces; sat on her stocking stuffed leg-like with rags, then
bullied us to pull, till off it flopped lolloping in our hands.

(Remembering this, I understand why my childhood dreams
were littered with dismembered limbs.) Her only certain things
were those amber glass door-pulls, and even they dissembled –
not jewels, or warm to touch, at times coming adrift in your mitts.

That parrot-cum-macaw Annie had Percy place down her yard,
behind the arch, so when you passed it squawked till ready to explode,
thrumming on its perch, some feather-weight warming for a punch.

Most of its joke was colour: bursts of scarlet, amber, gold that
blazed against gate of Sherwood-green and lime-washed wall –
Brazil in England. Try as he might, Percy couldn't make it talk.
Once he'd belted it so it never pecked his hands, but if strangers
leant to stroke, it squared them in the eye, crocked head – once,
twice – then struck. I dared it once: my sisters stared on petrified.

When Great Annie died, Micawber went (not dead, just sold)
and Percy took up bulldogs, thumping their plug-ugly weight
to rectangled coffee-tables with Queen Anne legs. True to form
they terrorized and grinned fixedly at their own gruesome jokes.

It must have been his job that made him fierce with things
at home. A placid man, he earned his keep for thirty years
and more by grinding down piles of bone to hoof and horn.

Even his nasturtiums – gleaming in scarlets, ambers, golds –
were bullied glorying up the wall, like parakeets among the white
and green. They never talked, or pecked, just held their mouths
in silent mocking grins: more dissembling jewels colding
to the touch, or coming adrift in uncertain mitts. Another joke?

There was this man named Percy, these flowers, and this poem…

Notes:

A Man There was Whose Alpha and Omega was Zed – In his diaries, Tchaikovsky denoted his homosexuality by the letter "Z". See J Gee & E Selby: *The Triumph of Tchaikovsky*

President for Life: Krk Island is in the former Yugoslavia.

Alderley Woods, November the First – 'I'm always surprised that so many poets choose to write about Spring and Autumn, subjects which have been so much written about that it must be extraordinarily difficult to say anything individual.' – Howard Sergeant, Bridport and District Arts Society Creative Writing Competition, October 1982

Game of Consequences and **Arms and A Boy** are part of the chain poem of 35 poems from 26 poets, ***A Game of Consequences,*** originated by Philip Gross. The full text with prose introduction appears in *Envoi* 111 (May 1995).